STUDENT BOOK 4

NATIONAL GEOGRAPHIC

EXPLORE OUR WORLD

SERIES EDITORS

JoAnn (Jodi) Crandall

Joan Kang Shin

AUTHORS

Kate Cory-Wright

Rob Sved

Australia • Brazil • Japan • Korea • Mexico • Singapore • Spain • United Kingdom • United States

NATIONAL GEOGRAPHIC

EXPLORE OUR WORLD

Let's sing! TR: 80

This is our world.
Everybody's got a song to sing.
Each boy and girl.
This is our world!

I say "our."
You say "world."
Our! World!
Our! World!

I say "boy."
You say "girl."
Boy! Girl!
Boy! Girl!

I say "Everybody move..."
I say "Everybody stop..."
Everybody stop!

This is our world.
Everybody's got a song to sing.
Each boy and girl.
This is our world!

Ha Long Bay, Vietnam

Unit 1

Feeling Fit

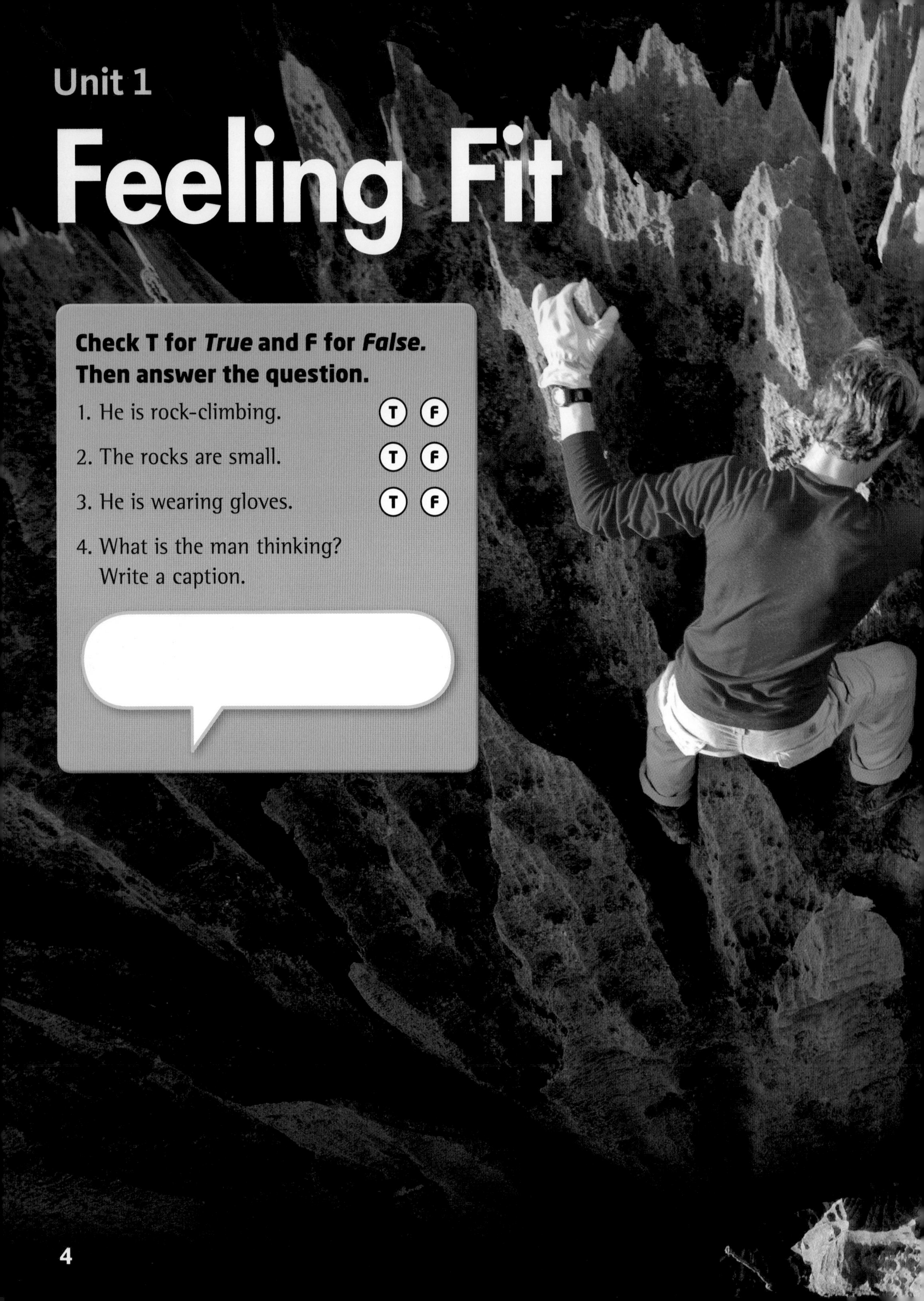

Check T for *True* and F for *False*. Then answer the question.

1. He is rock-climbing. (T) (F)
2. The rocks are small. (T) (F)
3. He is wearing gloves. (T) (F)
4. What is the man thinking? Write a caption.

Climbing the tsingy in Madagascar. Tsingy means "Where you cannot walk barefoot."

1 Listen and read. TR: 2

2 Listen and repeat. TR: 3

It's important to take care of your body. Exercise and good food help keep you fit and healthy.

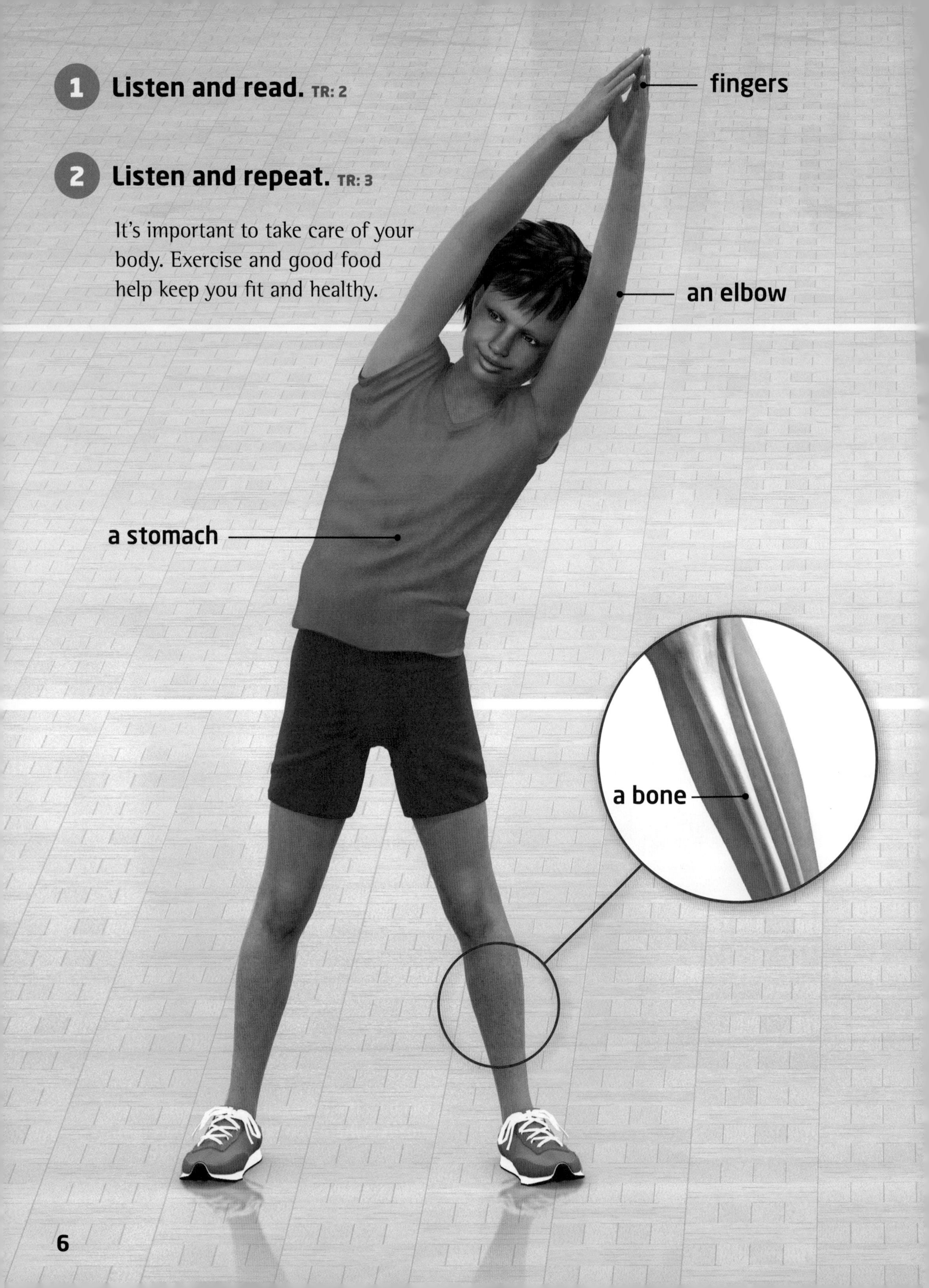

3 **Work with a partner.** Say, listen, and do.

GRAMMAR TR: 4

Did you **wash** your hands?	Yes, I **did.**
Did you **brush** your teeth?	No, I **didn't.**
Did he **take** a shower?	Yes, he **did.**

4 **Play a game.** Play with a partner. Take turns. Spin and ask questions.

5 **Listen and repeat.** Read and write. TR: 5

get exercise

eat junk food

eat vegetables

get rest

eat fruit

1. I ______________________ every day. I like apples, mangoes, and grapes!

2. I ______________________ every day. I play soccer and go swimming.

3. I ______________________ every day. I love carrots, beans, and potatoes.

4. I ______________________ every day. I relax after exercise, and I sleep at night!

5. I ______________________ sometimes. I eat potato chips and drink soda.

6 **Stick in order (1 = most important).** Work with a partner. Talk about what you think is important.

My number one is exercise. It's very important to get exercise.

My number one is fruit. I think it's important to eat fruit.

1	2	3	4	5

GRAMMAR TR: 6

It's important to get **enough** sleep. Don't stay up **too** late.
I drink **enough** water. I don't eat **too** much junk food.

7 **Read and make true sentences about you.** Underline the words.

1. I **drink / don't drink** too much soda.
2. I **get / don't get** enough exercise.
3. I **drink / don't drink** enough water.
4. I **eat / don't eat** too many chips.
5. I **watch / don't watch** too much TV.
6. I **get / don't get** enough sleep.

8 **Play a game.** Cut out the cards on page 97. Choose a card and flip a coin. Play with a partner.

Heads = good for you

Tails = bad for you

Tails. I watch too much TV. No points for me! Your turn.
Heads. I get enough sleep. One point for me!

9 Listen, read, and sing. TR: 7

Let's Move

We want to feel healthy.
We want to feel fit.
Come on, everybody.
Stand! Don't sit!

What did you do to be fit today?
What did you do to be strong?
What did you do to be fit today?
What did you do?

THE SOUNDS OF ENGLISH TR: 8

shoe

10 Listen and say.

1. shoulder shower
2. brush wash
3. vacation sugar

11 Listen and read. TR: 9

Get Rest *and* Exercise!

In some video games, you only sit on the sofa and play. This is fun, but you don't get much exercise. In other video games, you have fun *and* you get exercise. In these games, you move your whole body! A camera records the way you move. You can dance, run, or pretend to play soccer and watch yourself on the screen. These video games are a great way to keep fit. They make your muscles strong, but you don't get enough fresh air. Why don't you play a real game of soccer outside with your friends?

12 Look and write. Write about exercise with video games.

Video game	How you play	Why is it good?	Why is it bad?
1.	Sit on the sofa and play. Press buttons with your fingers.		
2.	Stand up and move. Watch yourself on the screen.		

weird but true You can control some video games with your brain!

Keep fit.
How do you keep fit?

Yosemite National Park, USA

Mireya Mayor
Primatologist/Conservationist
Emerging Explorer

"My job involves either chasing animals or running from animals chasing me, so staying fit is essential to doing work in my field!"

Unit 2

Let's Celebrate!

Look and check.

1. Holi is a festival of
   - ◯ food.
   - ◯ colors.
2. Someone is playing
   - ◯ a guitar.
   - ◯ a drum.
3. Would you like to go to this festival?
   - ◯ yes
   - ◯ maybe
   - ◯ no

Holi Festival, India

2 Listen and repeat. TR: 11

People all over the world have special celebrations. People **celebrate** their birthdays, the first day of the year, food, colors, and light. They wear **costumes** and **masks.** They **dance,** eat food, and sometimes watch a **parade.** Celebrations are fun!

a costume

a mask

a lantern

a party

fireworks

3 Work with a partner. Ask and answer.

Do you like to dress up?
Yes, I do. I have many costumes.

GRAMMAR TR: 12

Did you **watch** the parade? Yes, I **watched** the parade.
Did you **dance** at the party? Yes, I **danced** at the party.

4 **Play a game.** Play with a partner. Ask and answer. Take turns.

Heads: Move 2 spaces.

Tails: Move 1 space.

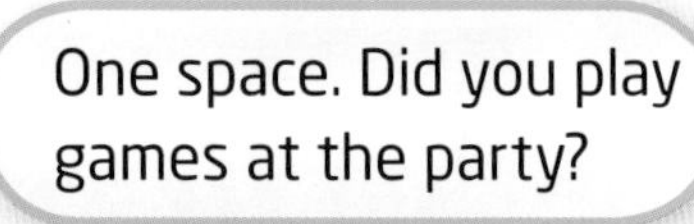

One space. Did you play games at the party?

Yes, we played games. It was fun.

5 **Listen and repeat.** Read and write. **TR: 13**

a birthday cake

candles

a present

an invitation

balloons

1. You write this on paper. You give it to your friends. ____________________

2. It tastes sweet. It usually has candles on top. ____________________

3. They are usually round. They have air inside. ____________________

4. They are long and thin. You put them on a birthday cake. ____________________

5. You wrap it. You give it to people on their birthdays. ____________________

6 **Listen and stick.** **TR: 14**

1	2	3	4	5

GRAMMAR TR: 15

Did you **go** to the parade?	Yes, I **went** to the parade.
Did you **see** the fireworks?	Yes, I **saw** the fireworks.
Did you **eat** cake at the party?	Yes, I **ate** a piece of cake at the party.

7 These verbs change when you talk about the past. Match. Draw lines.

sing	wrote
drink	gave
wear	had
have	took
write	sang
give	drank
take	wore

8 Play a game. Cut out the cards on page 99. Play with a partner. Match and say sentences.

See. Saw. I saw lots of lanterns. Your turn.
No match for me. Your turn again.
see
saw
have
drank

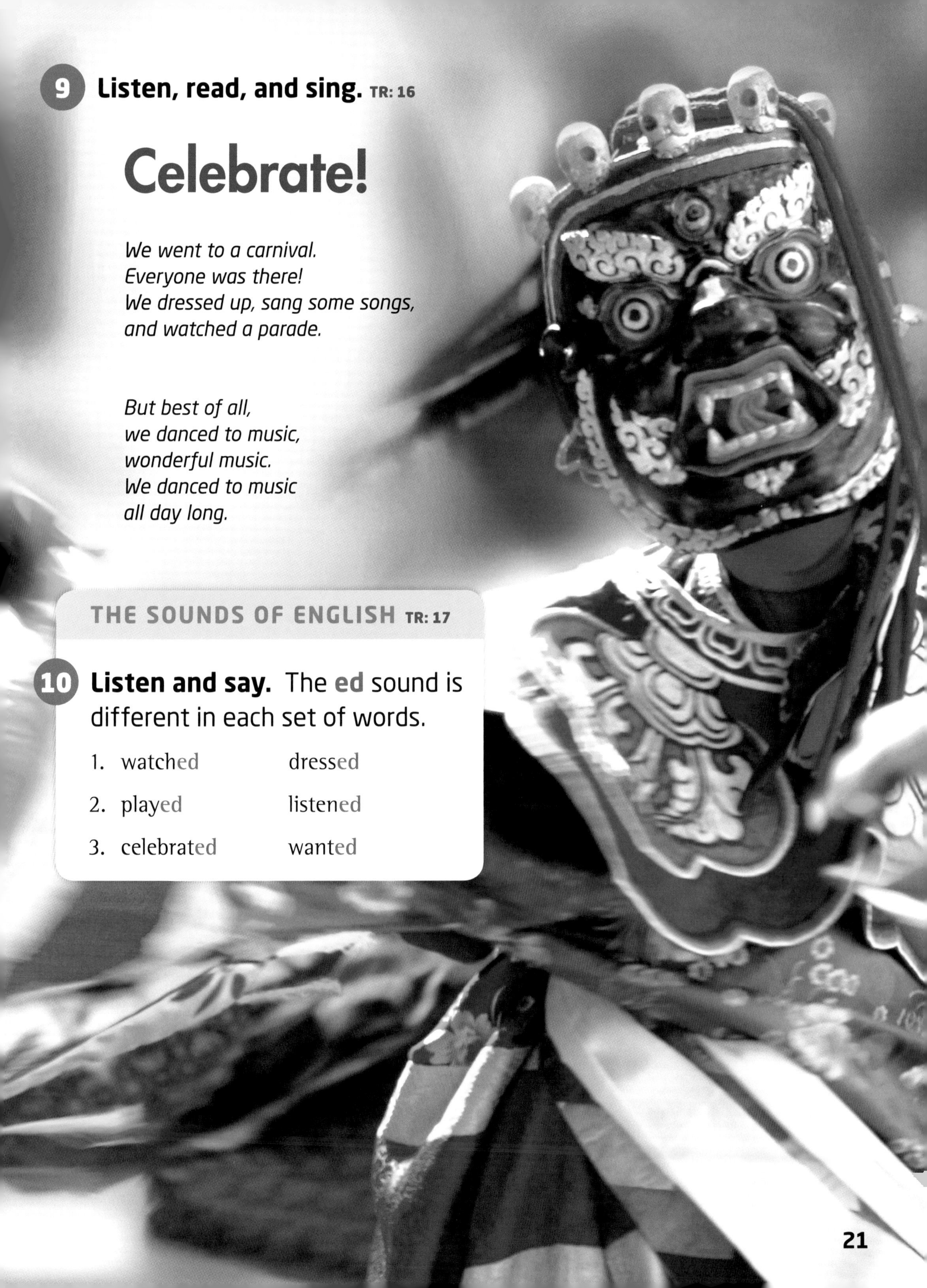

9 **Listen, read, and sing.** TR: 16

Celebrate!

We went to a carnival.
Everyone was there!
We dressed up, sang some songs,
and watched a parade.

But best of all,
we danced to music,
wonderful music.
We danced to music
all day long.

THE SOUNDS OF ENGLISH TR: 17

10 **Listen and say.** The **ed** sound is different in each set of words.

1. watched dressed
2. played listened
3. celebrated wanted

11 Listen and read. TR: 18

November Celebration

The Day of the Dead is an important festival in Mexico. People celebrate it on the first day of November.

Families take food to cemeteries, and they light candles and play music. Sometimes there are fireworks, too. People give candy and chocolate in the shape of skulls. For Mexicans, the festival is not sad. The Day of the Dead is a happy time.

Day of the Dead

12 **Read.** Complete the chart.

The Day of the Dead	
Where do people celebrate it?	
When is it?	
What do people do?	

In 2002, a candy company made chocolate fireworks! 60 kg (132 lb.) of chocolate went up into the sky!

13 **Talk with a partner.** Look at the pictures on this page. What do you see? What do you like?

I like the candles. I think they're beautiful.

I like the candles, too! And did you see those skulls?

Learn more about other cultures.

How do you learn more about other cultures?

Inti Raymi, Festival of the Sun, Cusco, Peru

Daniel Torres Etayo
Archaeologist
Emerging Explorer

"When I was a child, my father told me hundreds of fantastic stories about the Inca, Maya, and Aztec Empires; the European conquerors; and Cuba's own indigenous peoples."

Unit 3

My Weekend

Look and check. Then answer the question.

1. The boy is
   - ◯ playing basketball.
   - ◯ playing volleyball.
   - ◯ playing soccer.
2. What is the boy thinking? Write a caption.

Tegucigalpa, Honduras

1 Listen and read. TR: 19

2 Listen and repeat. TR: 20

The weekend is a time to relax and do fun things. Sometimes we stay home. We do our homework, play games, text our friends, and watch TV. Other times we go out and visit interesting places, play outside, or see friends. It's nice to keep busy! What do you do on weekends?

3 Work with a partner. Ask and answer.

What do you do on weekends?

Sometimes I go to the movies. How about you?

GRAMMAR TR: 21

How was your weekend?	It was boring. I **didn't do** anything special.
What did you do?	I went to a soccer game.
Did your team win?	No, they **didn't win.** They lost.

4 **Listen.** Underline the answer. TR: 22

What did you do on the weekend?

1. We **went / didn't go** on a picnic.

2. I **went / didn't go** to the movies.

3. We **won / didn't win** the basketball game.

4. I **watched / didn't watch** TV.

5 **Work in a small group.** Take a survey. Ask and answer. Tell about your weekend.

Name	stay home	text friends	go to the movies	watch TV	win a game

Did you stay home on the weekend?
No, I didn't. What about you?

6 **Listen and repeat.** Read and write. TR: 23

go horseback riding

go fishing

go hiking

go swimming

go ice skating

1. I ______________________ in the winter. I can go fast on the ice.
2. I ______________________ with my Dad. We don't catch many fish!
3. I ______________________ sometimes. Horses can run very fast.
4. I ______________________ with my family. We go into the woods.
5. I ______________________ every weekend. I can swim very well now.

7 **Stick your favorite activities.** Work with a partner. Ask and answer.

Do you want to go fishing?

No, I don't. I want to go hiking.

1	2	3	4	5

GRAMMAR TR: 24

What **did** you **do** last weekend?

We **didn't go hiking.**
We **went swimming.**

8 Look and write.

What did Carlos do on the weekend?

1. He went ice skating.
2. ______________________
3. ______________________
4. ______________________
5. ______________________

9 Play a game. Cut out the game board on page 101.

Play with a partner. Take turns. Flip a coin.

Heads: Yes + move one space

Tails: No

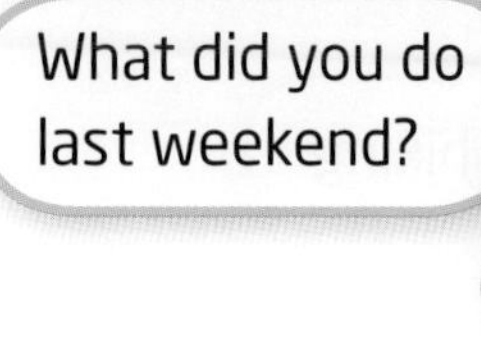
What did you do last weekend?

I didn't go to a party.

10 Listen, read, and sing. TR: 25

Free Time

What did you do on your weekend?
Did you stay at home? Did you have some fun?
What did you do on your weekend?
Did you go outside and play in the sun?

Did you go fishing?
Did you play baseball?
Did you go walking?
What did you do?

THE SOUNDS OF ENGLISH TR: 26

water

11 **Listen.** Underline the words that have a sound like the *w* in *water.*

1. How was your weekend?
2. What did you do?
3. Did you go walking?
4. Where did you go?

12 Listen and read. TR: 27

Wow! Look at That!

At The Children's Museum in Indianapolis, USA, there are giant models of dinosaurs outside. Some of them are running away, and others are looking in through the window! It's very exciting!

Inside the museum, you can go to the theater, learn about the stars in the planetarium, and go rock climbing. You can even celebrate your birthday there!

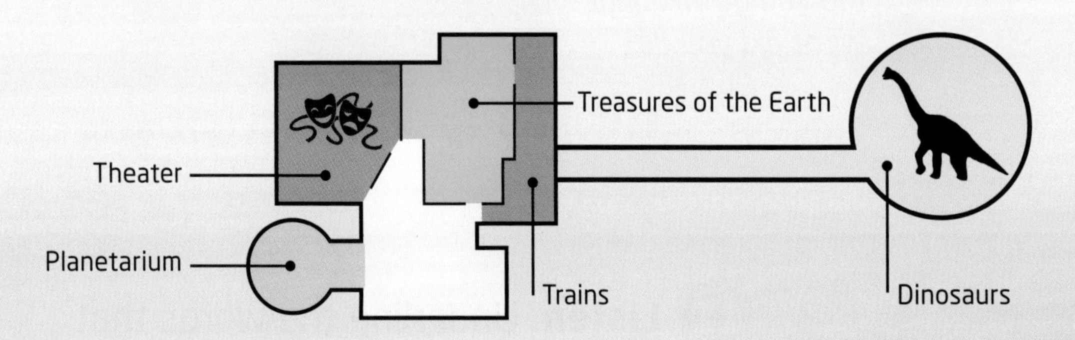

13 Work with a partner. Talk about the museum. Take turns. Ask and answer questions.

Did you like the museum?
Yes, I did. I saw dinosaurs!
weird but true
In Turkey, there is a museum of hair. It has hair from more than 16,000 people!

Try new things.

What new things would you like to learn to do?

NATIONAL GEOGRAPHIC

Iain Couzin
Behavioral Ecologist
Emerging Explorer

"I never had special training in math or computer science, but I realized the power of using computational tools, so I basically taught myself programming."

Unit 4

All in Our Family

Look and answer.

1. What is the girl holding?
2. Who are the other people in the photo?
3. How many family words do you know? Make a list.

1 Listen and read. TR: 28

2 Listen and repeat. TR: 29

Hi, I'm Andrea Martinez. Here we are at the Martinez family picnic. All my **relatives** are here. We're a big family. Some of us look the same. Some of us are very **different.** Our pets are different, too. My dog Roxy is **cuter** than my cousin's dog. Roxy is also **smarter** and **friendlier.**

older
younger

taller

shorter

3 **What did you learn?** How are the people different? Discuss with a partner.

Which dog is friendlier?

Roxy is friendlier.

GRAMMAR TR: 30

My best friend is **bigger** than I am.
My dog is **friendlier** than your cat.

I'm **shorter** than my sister.
Cats are **cuter** than dogs.

4 **Compare.** Work with a partner. Talk about the photos. Use words from the box.

tall	short	big	small
friendly	cute	old	young

5 **Work in a group.** Take turns. How are you and your relatives different?

I'm taller than my cousin, and older, too.
I'm friendlier than my sisters.

6 **Listen and repeat.** Look at the pictures. Match. TR: 31

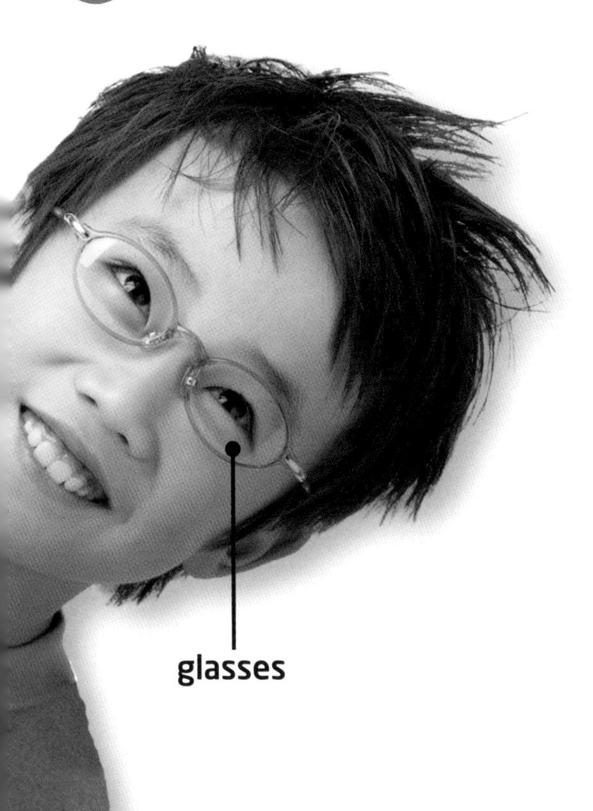

wavy hair

blond hair

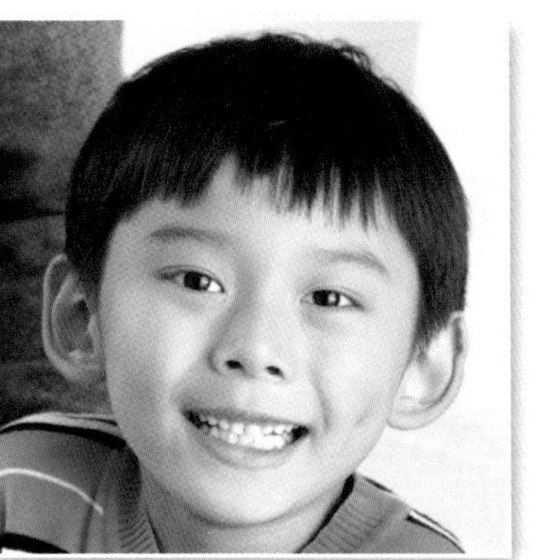

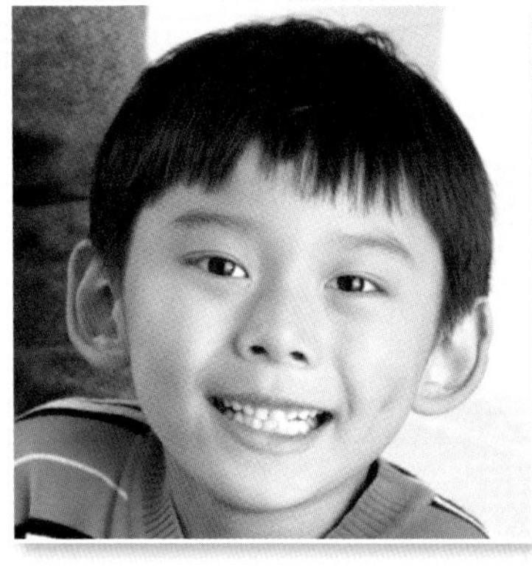

straight hair

curly hair

1. She looks just like her mother.
2. My cousin is really cute.
3. My cousins are very different.
4. My brother has blue eyes like me.

a. But he wears glasses, and I don't.
b. They both have straight hair.
c. I love his wavy hair.
d. But they both have curly hair.

7 **Listen and stick.** Work with a partner. Talk about you. TR: 32

He has brown hair.
I have brown hair, too.

She wears glasses.
I don't!

1	2	3	4	5

GRAMMAR TR: 33

What **are** you **doing** on Saturday? I'**m visiting** my aunt.
What **are** they **doing** at 7:00? They'**re having** dinner with their neighbors.

8 **Read.** Complete the sentences. Use the correct form of the word in parentheses.

1. Where ______________ you ______________ after school? (go)
2. What ______________ you ______________ on Saturday? (do)
3. ______________ you ______________ your relatives on the weekend? (visit)
4. ______________ you ______________ dinner with your family tonight? (have)

9 **Work with a partner.** Ask and answer the questions in Activity 8.

10 **Play a game.** Cut out the cards on page 103. Play with a partner. Listen, talk, and act it out.

Guess what I'm doing after lunch?
After lunch you're playing soccer.

11 Listen, read, and sing. TR: 34

We're All Different

I'm taller than you.
He's taller than me.
We're all different.
Yes, we're different.
And I like being me!

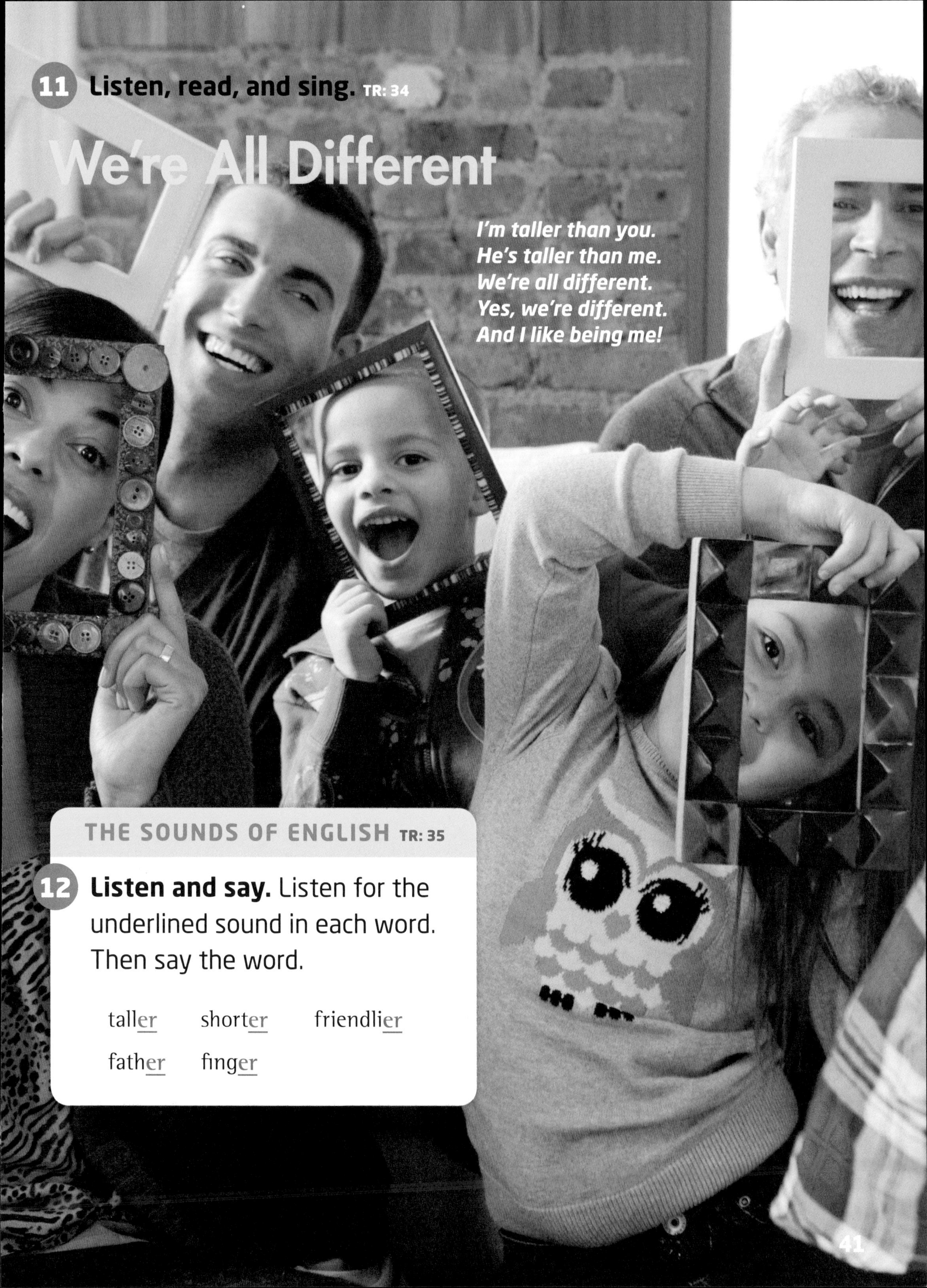

THE SOUNDS OF ENGLISH TR: 35

12 Listen and say. Listen for the underlined sound in each word. Then say the word.

tall<u>er</u> short<u>er</u> friendli<u>er</u>
fath<u>er</u> fing<u>er</u>

13 **Listen and read.** TR: 36

Where Do Your Eyes Come From?

The color of your eyes and your hair come from your family. We call them family traits. How tall you are, the shape of your face, and even the shape of your ears are all family traits.

EYE COLOR	
most common	
second most common	
rarest	

You inherit other traits from your family, too. For example, how do you fold your hands? Do you cross your right thumb over your left thumb? Or do you cross your left thumb over your right thumb? Now ask your parents to fold their hands! It's fun to look at these traits with your family and friends. Try it!

right thumb over left thumb

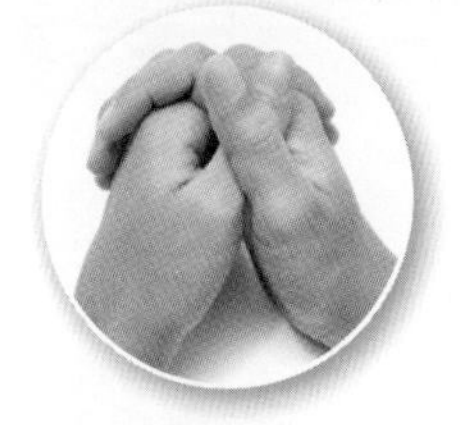

Blonds have more hairs on their heads than people with brown hair do.

14 **Work with a partner.** Choose three traits in the box below. Who did you inherit these traits from? Discuss.

eye color	nose shape
hair color	shape of face
type of hair	

I have straight, dark hair. My mother has straight, dark hair, too.

Understand the human family.

Are all the people in the world one big family? How are they the same? How are they different?

Spencer Wells
Geneticist
Emerging Explorer

"Everyone alive today descends from one woman who lived around 180,000 years ago."

Review

1 **Listen.** Check activities that the boy did on the weekend. **TR: 37**

☐ ☐ ☐ ☐

2 **Read and write.** Complete the sentences. Use the words in the box.

went	didn't go	lost	didn't lose
rode	didn't ride	got	didn't get
played	didn't play	won	didn't win

1. On Saturday I ______________ on a picnic because it was raining!
2. I ______________ my bike because the weather was bad.
3. I stayed home all day, so I ______________ enough exercise!
4. On Sunday the weather was great, so I ______________ soccer with my friends.
5. We ______________ the game. We lost!
6. We played another game. This time we ______________ the game. We won!

3 **Work with a partner.** Take turns. Ask and answer questions about your weekend.

How was your weekend?
It was exciting!
What did you do?
I went to the movies on Saturday. On Sunday I went on a picnic with my family.

4 **Work in a group.** Take turns. Ask and answer questions about your family. Take notes.

1. How many brothers and sisters do you have?
2. Are they older or younger than you?
3. Are you taller than some of your relatives? Who?
4. Do most people in your family have straight, curly, or wavy hair?
5. Who wears glasses in your family?
6. Tell how two people in your family are the same and different.

5 **Work in a group.** Compare your information.

I have one brother. He's older than me.

I have two younger sisters.

Me, too!

6 **Write.** You are making plans for a birthday party. Write who is doing each activity. Use the information in the box below.

I / send / invitations
My aunt / make / my birthday cake
Dad / prepare the fireworks
Mom and Dad / buy / my present
Grandma / make / my costume

In my family, we're planning my birthday party. I'm sending the invitations. My aunt . . .

Hello!

I will . . .
- greet people (formally and informally).
- say thank you (formally and informally).

1 Listen and read. TR: 38

Sofia: **Hello,** Mrs. Gomez. **How are you?**
Mrs. Gomez: **I'm very well, thank you,** Sofia. Please come in.
Sofia: Thank you.

Sofia: **Hi,** Carla! **What's up?**
Carla: **Not much.** Hey, do you want a soda?
Sofia: Sure! **Thanks.**

Hello. Good morning. Good afternoon. Good evening.	**How are you?** How are you today?	**I'm very well, thank you.** I'm fine, **thanks.**
Hi! Hi there! Hey!	**What's up?** What are you doing? How's it going?	**Not much.** Nothing. Fine. Not bad.

2 **Work with a partner.** Greet each other. Use the chart. Take turns.

What does that mean?

I will . . .
- interrupt someone (formally and informally).
- ask the meaning and ask how to spell or say something.
- explain a meaning and give a spelling.
- say that I don't know.

3 Listen and read. TR: 39

Antoni: **Hey,** Martina, **what does this mean?**

Martina: **I don't know. I think it's a kind of** exercise.

Antoni: I'm not sure. Let's ask the teacher.

Martina: **That's a good idea. Excuse me,** Ms. Biga.
What does this word mean?

Hey, **Excuse me, Mr. / Ms. / Mrs. ________.**	**What does ________ mean?**	**I think it's a kind of ________.** I think it means ________. It's the opposite of ________.	**I don't know.** I'm not sure.	**That's a good idea.** Good point.
	How do you spell ________? How do you pronounce this word? How do you say ________?			

4 Listen. You will hear two discussions. Read each question and circle the answer. TR: 40

1. What does the boy want to know?
   a. meaning b. spelling c. pronunciation

2. What does the girl want to know?
   a. meaning b. spelling c. pronunciation

5 Work in pairs. Prepare and practice discussions. You want to know the spelling, the meaning, or the pronunciation of a word. Ask your partner and then ask the teacher.

Unit 5

Fresh Food

Look and answer.

1. What are the people buying and selling?
2. How is this market different from the places where your family buys food?
3. How many fruits and vegetables in the photo can you name?

Floating market, Damnoen Saduak, Thailand

1 Listen and read. TR: 41

2 Listen and repeat. TR: 42

Every week many people go to the supermarket to buy vegetables like **cabbages** and **pumpkins.** These vegetables come from big farms. People like to go to the supermarket because it's easy and it's quick. But some people prefer to **grow** their own vegetables. For example, they grow **onions,** carrots, and **cucumbers.**

It's easier than you think to grow vegetables. First, you **dig.** Then you **plant** the seeds. Then, when the vegetables are ready, you can **pick** them. But you have to take care of your garden. Vegetables need water and sun. And sometimes insects eat your **lettuce!**

3 **Work with a partner.** What did you learn? Ask and answer.

Why do people grow their own vegetables?
Because it's easy!

GRAMMAR TR: 43

I **have to** wash and cut the vegetables.

I **don't have to** buy any more seeds.

She **has to** plant the tomatoes in a sunny place.

He **doesn't have to** do homework today.

4 **What about you?** Write five things you usually have to do.

In the morning I ______________________________.

In the afternoon I ______________________________.

In the evening I ______________________________.

On weekends I ______________________________.

On Sunday I ______________________________.

5 **Play a game.** Cut out the cubes on page 105. Work with a partner. Ask and answer.

Morning. Eat lunch. Do you have to eat lunch in the morning?
morning

No. I don't have to eat lunch in the morning. I have to eat lunch in the afternoon.

6 **Listen and say.** Read and write about what you do. TR: 44

How often?

S	M	T	W	T	F	S
do homework eat fruit	eat fruit	do homework eat fruit	eat fruit	do homework eat fruit	go to market eat fruit	eat fruit
do homework eat fruit	eat fruit	do homework eat fruit	eat fruit	do homework eat fruit	go to market eat fruit	take vegetables to Sue eat fruit
do homework eat fruit	eat fruit	do homework eat fruit	eat fruit	do homework eat fruit	go to market eat fruit	eat fru
do homework eat fruit	eat fruit	do homework eat fruit	eat fruit	do homework eat fruit	go to market eat fruit	plant ea plant

every day → eat fruit

on (Fridays) → go to market

once (a month) → take vegetables to Sue

three times (a week) → do homework

twice (a year) → plant

1. Every day I ______________________________.

2. On Fridays I ______________________________.

3. Three times a week I ______________________________.

4. Twice a year we ______________________________.

5. Once a month we ______________________________.

7 **Work with a partner.** Ask and answer, and then stick.

How often do you ride your bike?

Twice a day.

1	2	3	4	5

GRAMMAR TR: 45

What **would** you **like** for lunch? I'**d like** a bowl of vegetable soup.

8 **Read.** Complete the dialogue.

A: Welcome to Mario's Café. What ___would you like___ to order today?

B: I ______________ some pumpkin soup and bread.

C: I ______________ some chicken and rice, please.

D: I usually order pie, but today I ______________ some ice cream.

9 **Play a game.** Play with a partner. Make sentences. Take turns.

Heads: Move 1 space.

Tails: Move 2 spaces.

10 Listen, read, and sing. TR: 46

Something's Growing

Pumpkin, lettuce, peppers, and beans.
Something's growing, and it's green.
Pumpkin, lettuce, peppers, and beans.
Something's growing, and it's green.

Working in the garden,
working in the sun,
working in the garden is a lot of fun.

THE SOUNDS OF ENGLISH TR: 47

banana

11 Listen and repeat.

1. about   around
2. tomato   potato
3. children   chicken

12 **Listen and read.** TR: 48

Up the Wall and On the Roof

Would you like to grow fruit and vegetables, but you don't have a big yard? Look up! There is lots of space! You can grow food up the walls or even on the roof!

Growing vegetables up a wall is easy. Choose a sunny place and choose plants that climb. Peas and tomatoes are good choices.

"Roof gardens" are great because you can grow lots of different vegetables and fruits. In one roof garden, a class of children grew 453 kg (1,000 pounds) of vegetables in one year. The children grew cabbages, carrots, lettuce, and even strawberries! They enjoyed the fresh food they grew in their outside classroom.

Below ground

Carrots

On the ground

Lettuce

Above ground

Tomatoes

weird but true

Most people spend about five years of their life eating.

13 **Work with a partner.** Imagine you have a roof garden. Talk about it.

We can plant carrots and lettuce in our garden.
It's fun to grow fresh vegetables!

Appreciate local food.

Why is it important to appreciate local food?

NATIONAL GEOGRAPHIC

Juan Martinez
Environmentalist
Emerging Explorer

"Learning how to grow jalapeños changed my life."

Unit 6

Long Ago and Today

Look and circle.

1. They are riding
   a. to school. b. to the market.
2. The boy is holding
   a. a box. b. a computer.

Look and answer.

3. What makes you think this photo is from the present?
4. What makes you think it's from the past?

Father and son biking to school, Uttar Pradesh, India

1 Listen and read. TR: 49

2 Listen and repeat. TR: 50

How did people **spend time** long ago? How were their days different from our days today? How were they the same?

Then

Life was very different for people all over the world two hundred years ago. How did people **begin** their day? They got up when the sun came up. There were no **electric lights,** so people did their **chores** during the day.

Their chores were different, too. To get hot water, for example, people had to **make** a **fire**. Families had to **learn** how to make soap and grow their own vegetables. They made their own clothes, too. And of course people had to **wash** dishes by hand because there were no machines.

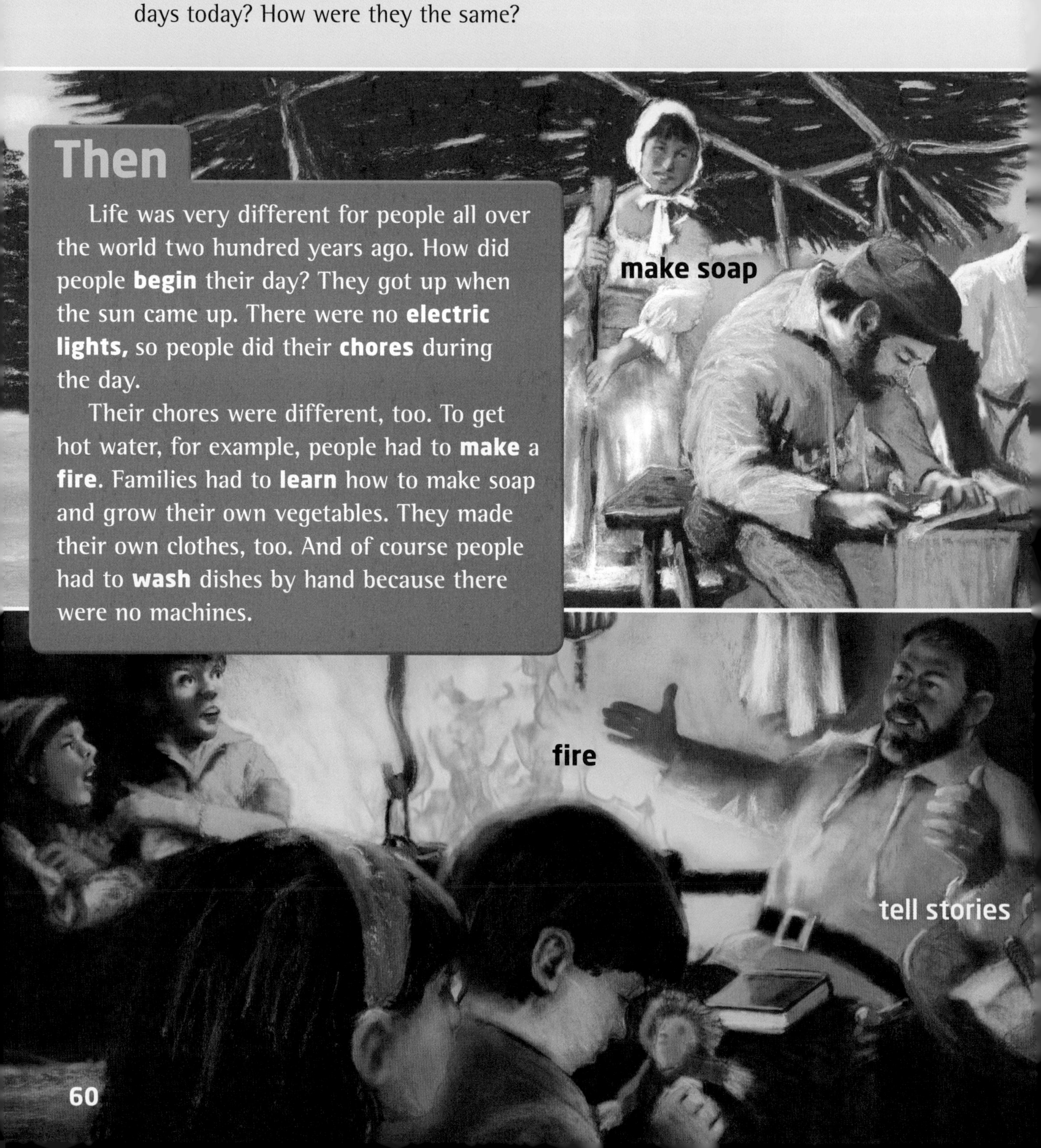

3 **Work with a partner.** What did you learn? Ask and answer.

Why did people get up with the sun?
They wanted to do their chores in the daytime. They didn't have electric lights.
cell phone
electric light

Now

Today most people in the world have electric lights and **cell phones.** People still have to do chores, but in their free time, they can watch TV, make calls, and play video games.

Of course, not everybody lives this way. Many families don't like to spend a lot of time in front of the computer or TV. They prefer to go hiking or go on picnics. At home they like to talk, **tell** stories, and play card games with their friends and family. What about you?

GRAMMAR TR: 51

Long ago, children walked to school, **but** I take the bus.
Two hundred years ago, people didn't have TV. They told stories **instead.**

4 **Same or different?** Write true sentences.

My grandparents . . .	Me
watched TV.	*I watch TV, too.*
grew their own vegetables.	*I buy vegetables in a store instead.*
walked everywhere.	
played board games.	
sent letters to their friends.	

5 **Work in a group.** Talk about your grandparents' lives and your life. How are they different?

My grandmother washed clothes by hand, but I use a washing machine instead!

6 **Listen and say.** Then read. Check **T** for *True* or **F** for *False*. TR: 52

1. Video games are modern toys. Ⓣ Ⓕ
2. Parents say that cleaning your room is an important chore. Ⓣ Ⓕ
3. A pencil eraser is expensive. Ⓣ Ⓕ
4. The telephone in the photo above is old-fashioned. Ⓣ Ⓕ
5. This sentence isn't difficult. Ⓣ Ⓕ

7 **Work with a partner.** Talk and stick.

Look at this. What do you think?

It's very expensive.

1	2	3	4	5

GRAMMAR TR: 53

Life was **more difficult** back then.
That cell phone is **more expensive than** this one.

8 Complete the sentences.

1. I think jumping rope is ______________________ (difficult) riding a bike.

2. Getting exercise is ______________________ (important) watching TV all day.

3. Video games are ______________________ (expensive) board games.

4. Board games are ______________________ (old-fashioned) video games, but they're fun to play.

5. Our new house is ______________________ (modern) our old one.

9 **Play a game.** Cut out the game board on page 107. Play with a partner. Make sentences about the pictures.

This phone is more old-fashioned than that one.
Heads: Move 1 space.
Tails: Move 2 spaces.
My turn!

10 Listen, read, and sing. TR: 54

Yesterday and Today

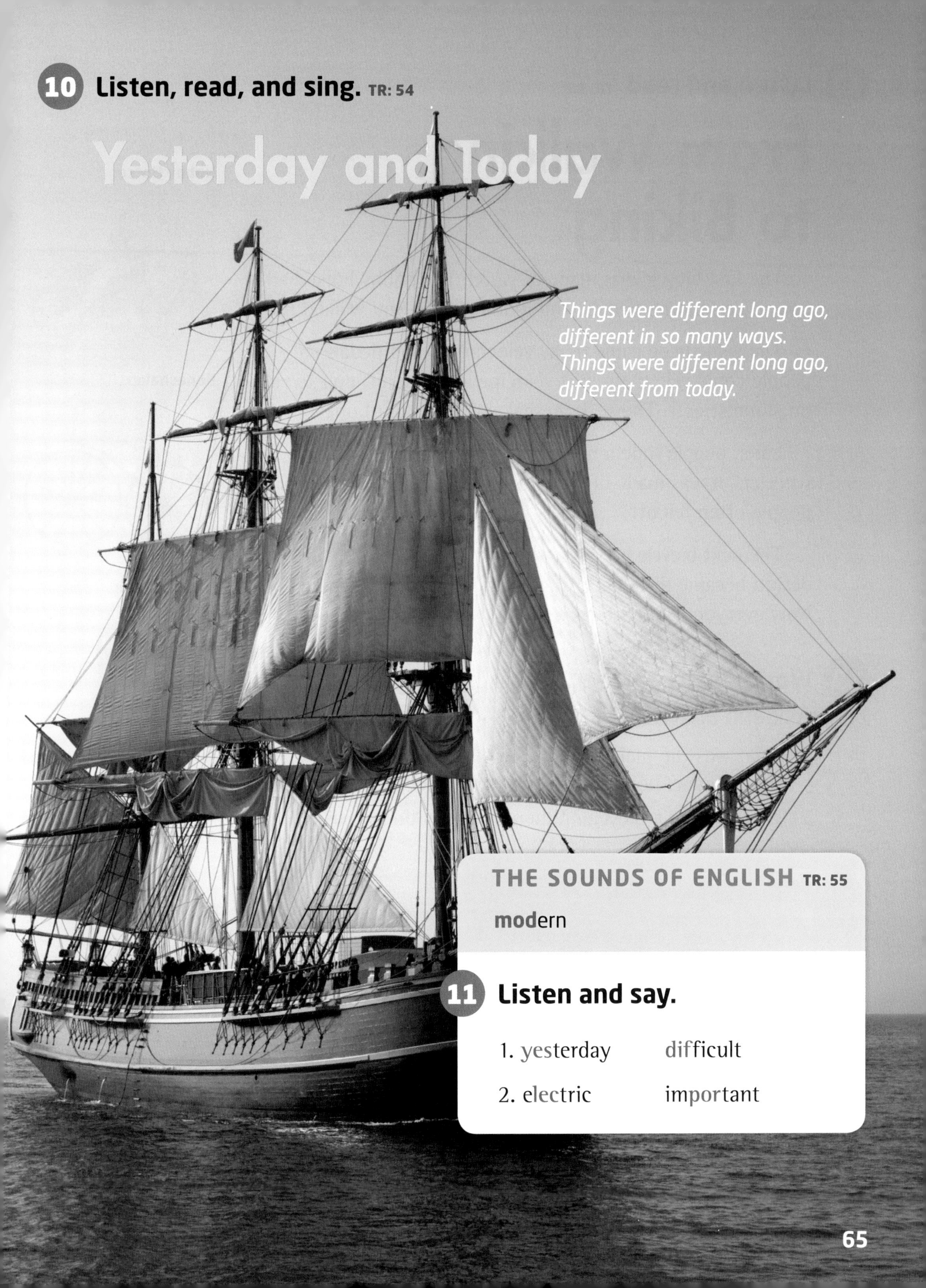

Things were different long ago,
different in so many ways.
Things were different long ago,
different from today.

THE SOUNDS OF ENGLISH TR: 55

modern

11 Listen and say.

1. **yes**terday — **dif**ficult
2. e**lec**tric — im**por**tant

12 **Listen and read.** TR: 56

From Walking to Biking

The first bicycle was made of wood. The hobby horse had two wheels but no pedals. You didn't ride it—you walked it!

The velocipede came next. Velocipedes had pedals so people could ride them. But velocipedes were difficult to ride on stone streets. These "boneshakers" hurt your bones!

Later, people rode a new kind of bicycle called a "high wheeler." It was made of metal and had a high front wheel so people often fell off!

The next bicycle had two wheels of the same size. This design became the standard for modern children's bicycles. Now everyone enjoys bicycles!

Hobby Horse

Boneshaker

High Wheeler

Children's Bicycle

13 **Work with a partner.** Talk about bicycles. Ask and answer.

1. What was the main problem with each kind of bicycle: hobby horse, boneshaker, and high wheeler?
2. Do you have a bicycle? When and how do you use it?
3. Why are bicycles a good idea?

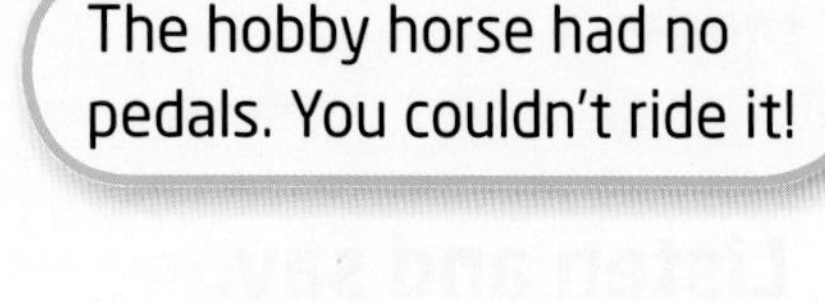

The hobby horse had no pedals. You couldn't ride it!

The longest bike ever made was about 36 m (117 ft.) long!

Appreciate the past.

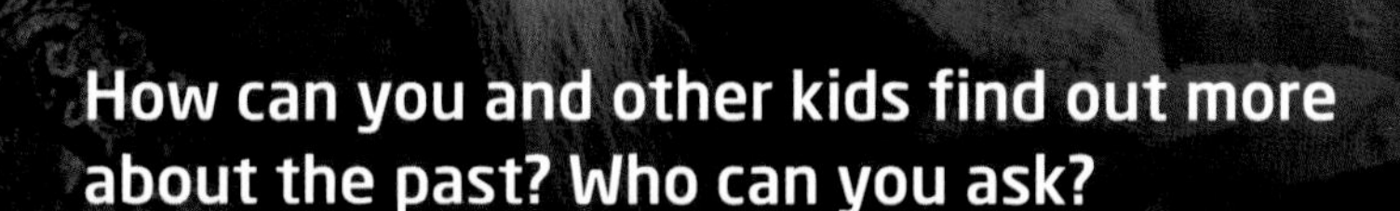

How can you and other kids find out more about the past? Who can you ask?

Stephen Ambrose (1936–2002)
Historian
Explorer-in-Residence Emeritus

"The past is a source of knowledge, and the future is a source of hope. Love of the past implies faith in the future."

Unit 7

Get Well Soon!

Look and answer.

1. What's the matter with her?
   She has ______________.
   - ◯ a cold
   - ◯ a broken arm
   - ◯ a headache
2. How do you think she feels?
   - ◯ It hurts a lot.
   - ◯ It hurts, but she feels fine.
   - ◯ Better than ever.
3. Write a speech bubble for this girl.

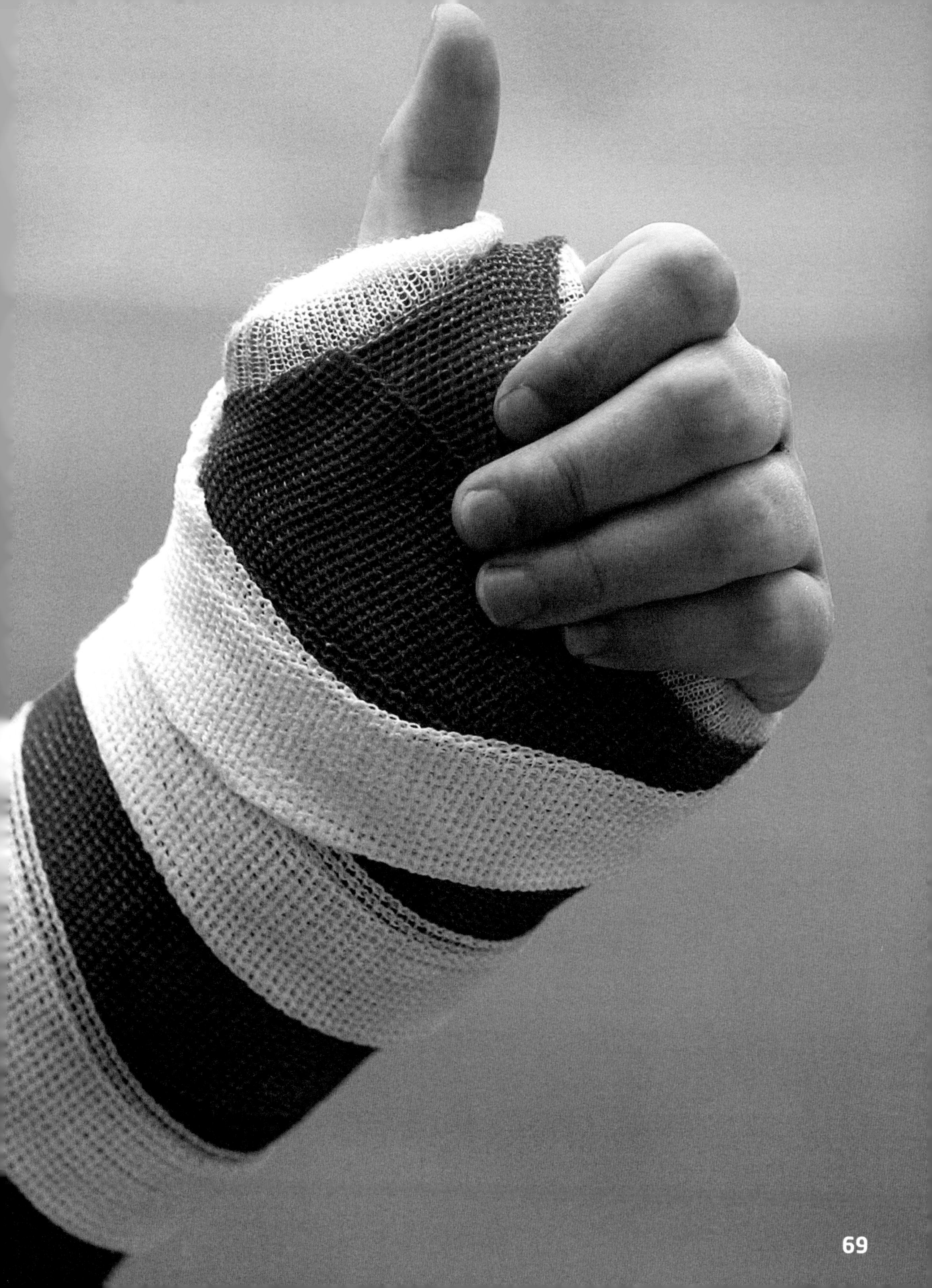

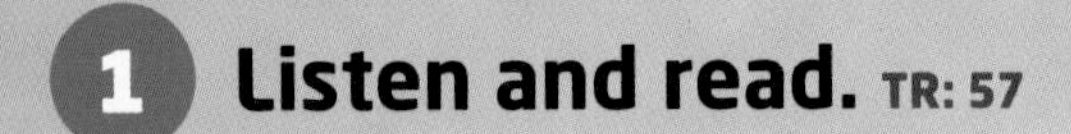

1 Listen and read. TR: 57

2 Listen and repeat. TR: 58

Our bodies are amazing. Every day they work hard to keep us healthy. But everyone gets sick sometimes. When you **have a cold** or you **have a fever,** it means germs entered your body. You can't see germs, but they can make you sick. Some germs can live for two hours on your desk. So use **tissues** when you **sneeze** or **cough!** And wash your hands with soap.

sneeze

a tissue

have a cold

an earache

Germs aren't the only things that can make you feel bad. You may get an **earache,** a **headache,** or a **stomachache.**

It's a good idea to have a **first-aid kit,** too. That's a good place to keep **medicine.**

3 Work with a partner. What did you learn? Ask and answer.

GRAMMAR TR: 59

I have a bad earache.
You **shouldn't** wait any longer.

What **should** I do?
Your mom **should** take you to the doctor.

4 **Work with a partner.** Look at the photos. Give advice. Use the words in the box.

use tissues	go out	go to the doctor
sneeze on people	go to bed	go to school

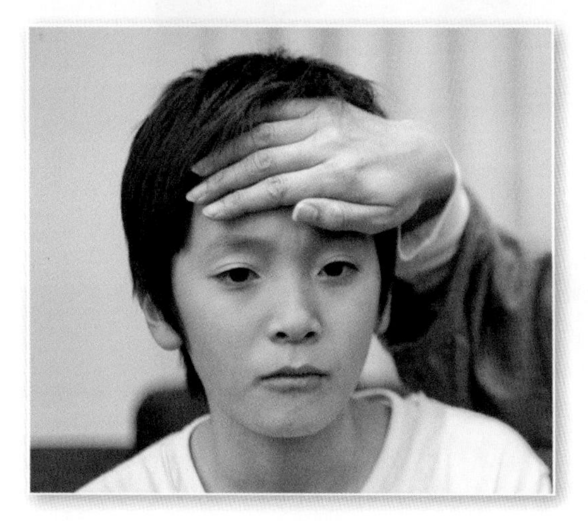

He feels sick. He has a fever.

She has a cold and a cough.

5 **Work in a group.** Act out an illness. Guess and give advice. Take turns.

6 **Listen and repeat.** Read and circle the letter. TR: 60

a broken leg

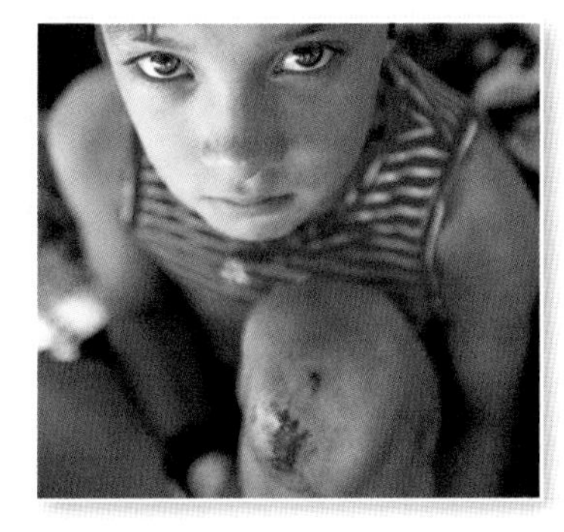

a scratch

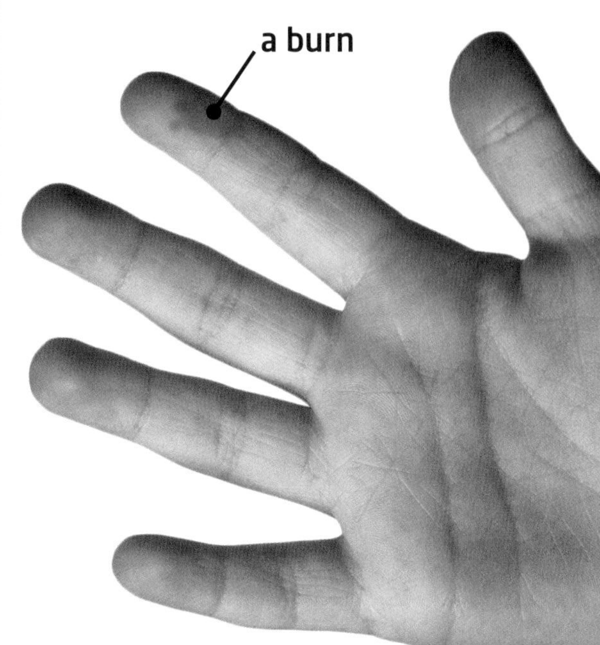

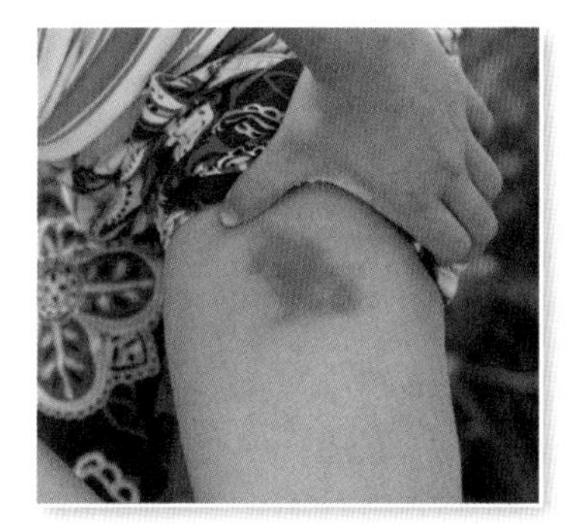

a bruise

a cut

1. Why can't you run? a. I have a broken leg. b. I have a bruise.
2. Is that a burn? a. Yes, I have a headache. b. Yes, I touched the stove!
3. I have a scratch. What should I do?
   a. You should wash it. b. You should go to bed.
4. What an ugly bruise. What happened to her?
   a. She had a bike accident. b. She ate too much chocolate.
5. How did you get that cut?
   a. I ran with scissors. Bad idea! b. I ate too much ice cream. Bad idea!

7 **Work with a partner.** Listen. Talk and stick. TR: 61

What happened on Monday?

His brother got a cut on his finger.

Monday	Tuesday	Wednesday	Thursday	Friday

GRAMMAR TR: 62

a cut ⟶ to cut
a burn ⟶ to burn

Ouch! I cut **myself.**
Be careful. Don't hurt **yourself.**
My brother burned **himself** on the stove. He shouldn't cook by **himself.**
Look at that bandage. Did she hurt **herself?**

8 **Read and write.** Complete the sentences.

1. Last week I ran with scissors and I fell. I cut ____________________.
2. When my sister touched the stove, she burned ____________________. It was terrible.
3. You are always sick! You should take care of ____________________.
4. My brother didn't listen to me, and he hurt ____________________.

9 **Play a game.** Cut out the cards on page 109. Glue the cards. Listen. TR: 63

1	2	3
4		5
6	7	8

10 **Listen, read, and sing.** TR: 64

Get Well Soon

Take care of yourself. You know what to do.
Exercise a lot and eat the right food.
But once in a while, when you don't feel well,
here are some things that you should do.

THE SOUNDS OF ENGLISH TR: 65

vet

11 **Listen and say.** Underline the *v* sound in each word.

vet	very	visit	vegetable
fever	every	relative	invitation

12 Listen and read. TR: 66

Why Do We Sneeze?

Aaaaa . . . choo! When you have a cold, you often sneeze. Why? Because germs make a home in your nose, and they tickle you! Sneezing is your body's way of sending germs out of your nose. Many animals sneeze, too!

What happens? Your nose doesn't like the germs, so it sends a message to a part of your brain called the "sneeze center." The sneeze center sends a message to your muscles. Then all your muscles push hard. Even your eyes push. That's why you close your eyes when you sneeze! You should have a tissue ready because the sneeze happens very quickly. A sneeze can travel as fast as a car!

A sneeze from one person on the subway can reach 150 other people.

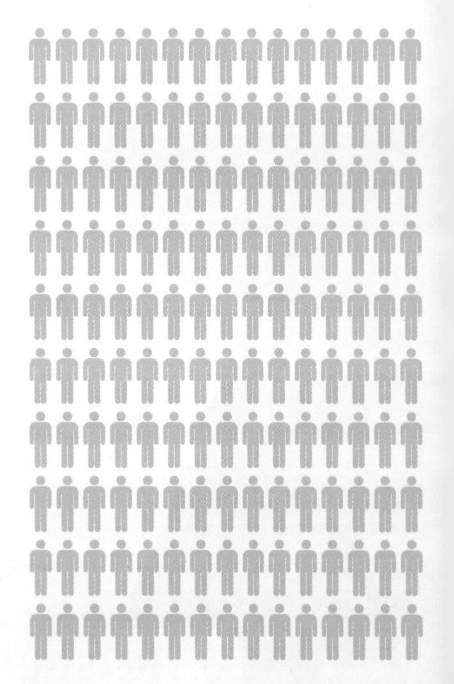

13 **Work with a partner.** Ask questions and take notes. Take turns.

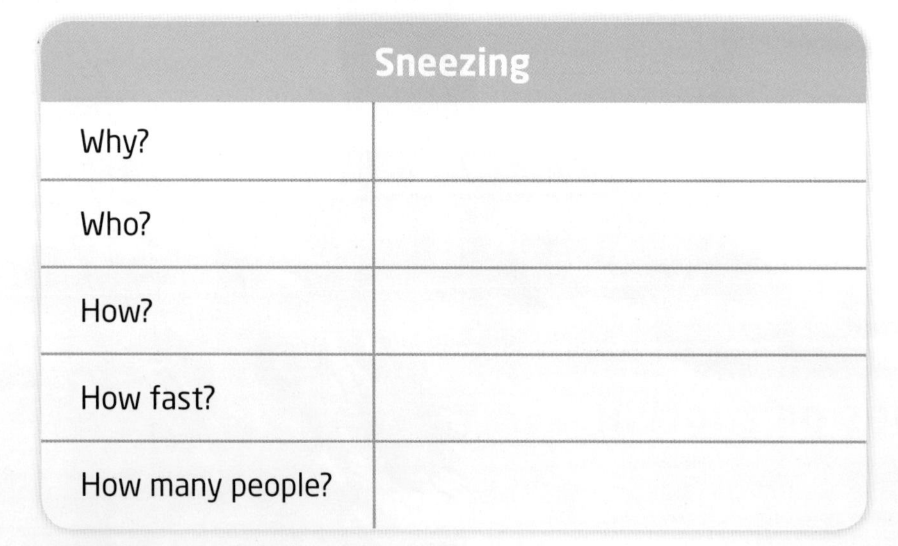

Sneezing	
Why?	
Who?	
How?	
How fast?	
How many people?	

Iguanas sneeze more than any other animal!

How many people can a sneeze reach?

It can reach 150 people.

Be prepared.

How can we be prepared for illness and accidents?

A rope rescue in Sedona, Arizona, USA

NATIONAL GEOGRAPHIC

Hayat Sindi, UNESCO Goodwill
Ambassador for Sciences
Emerging Explorer

"My mission is to find simple, inexpensive ways to check on the health of people in distant places and difficult conditions."

Unit 8

My Favorites

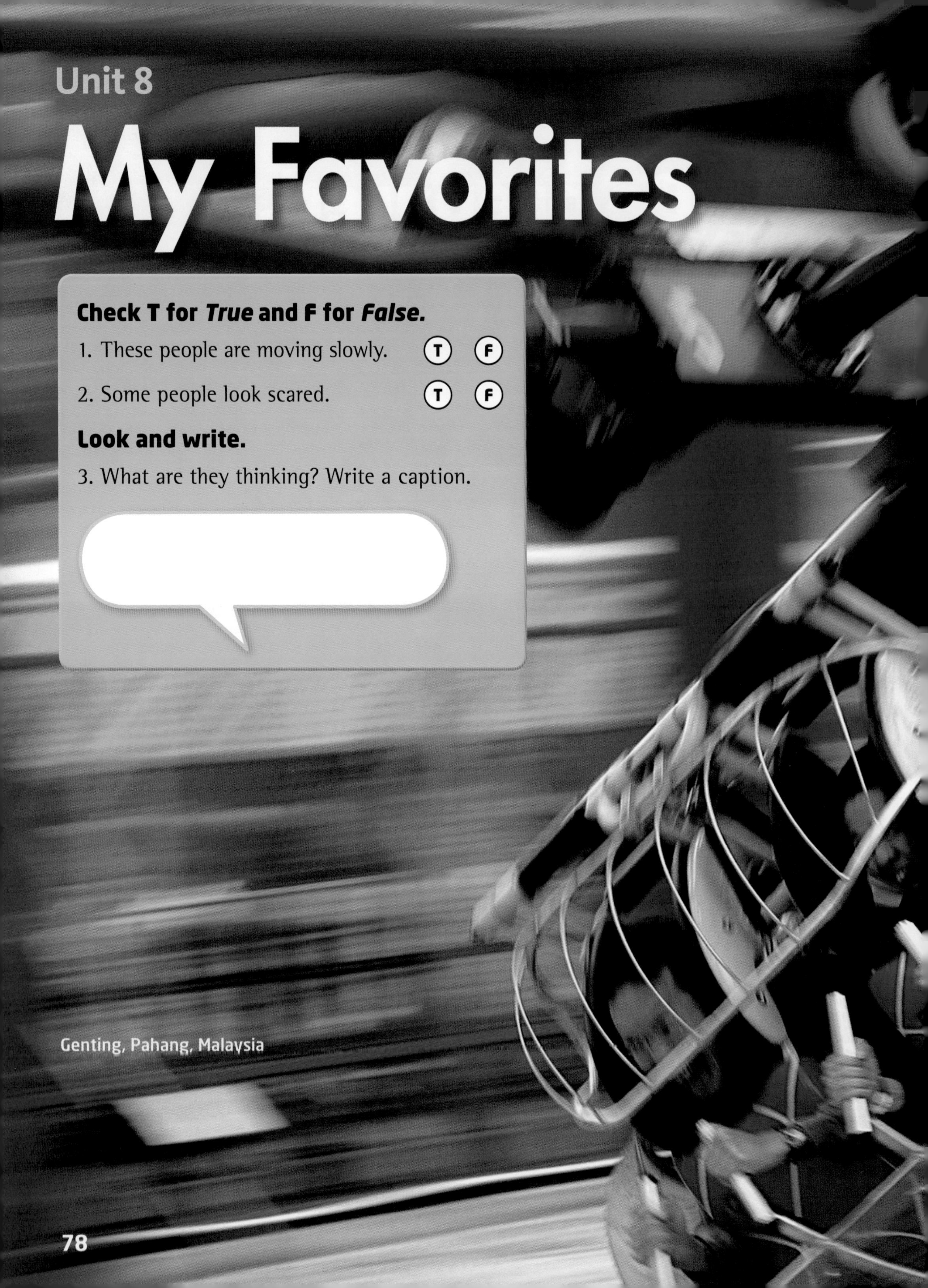

Check T for *True* and F for *False*.

1. These people are moving slowly. T F
2. Some people look scared. T F

Look and write.

3. What are they thinking? Write a caption.

Genting, Pahang, Malaysia

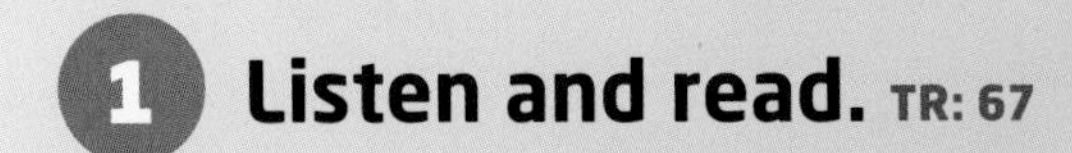

1 **Listen and read.** TR: 67

2 **Listen and repeat.** TR: 68

Wax museums are **amazing.** You can see hundreds of **famous** people. The people aren't real, but they look real!

In these **cool** museums, you can say "Hi" to all your favorite **actors** and **popular** TV stars. You can *hear* some of them, too! Meet a singer or actor from a **funny movie.** Take photos with a famous **person** or stand next to an **athlete** like Yao Ming. He's **great.**

There are interesting characters from history, too, like Cleopatra and Genghis Khan!

Cleopatra, Courtesy of the Wax Museum of Madrid

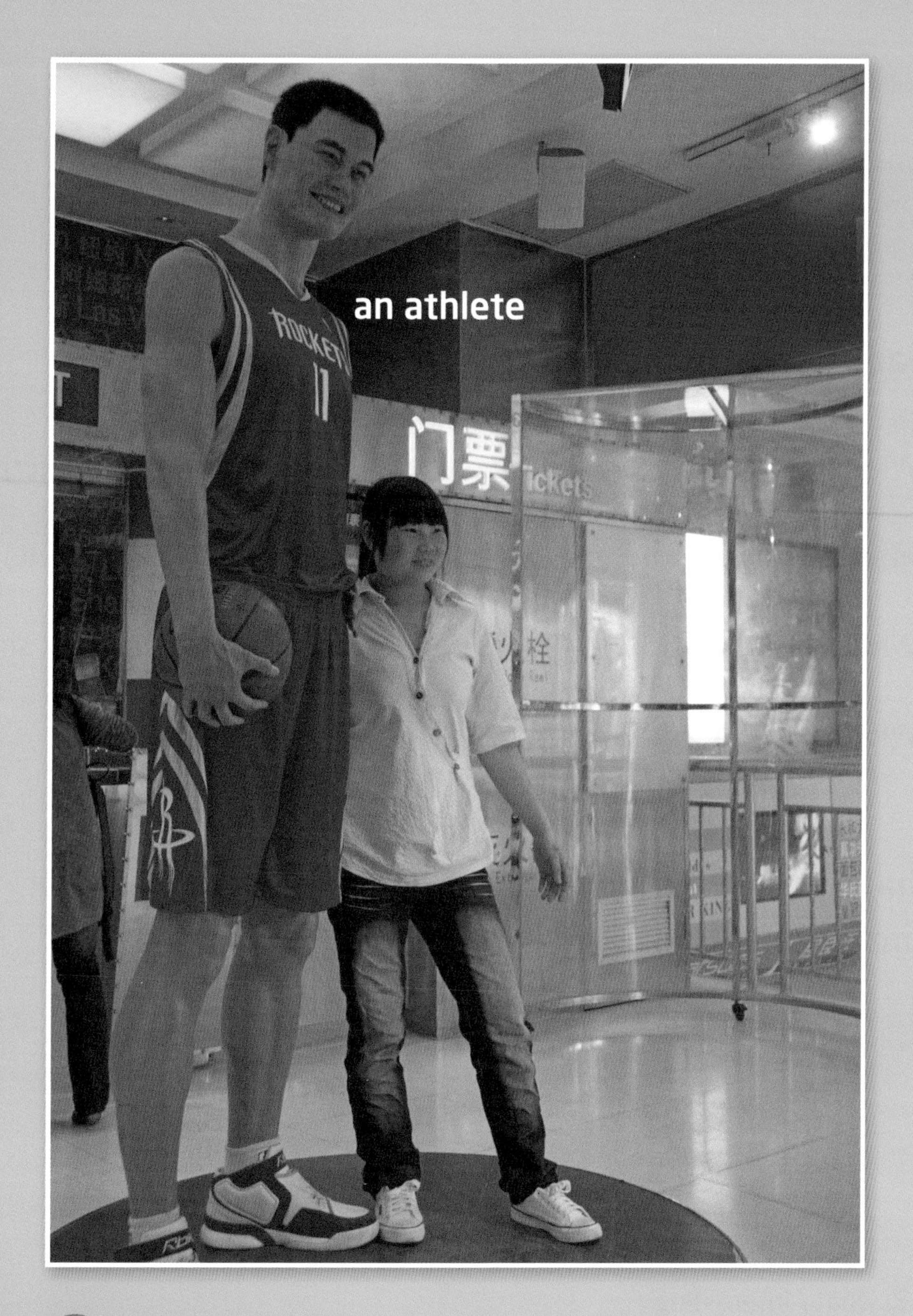

3 **Work with a partner.** What did you learn? Ask and answer.

Can you see athletes in the museum?
Yes, you can. Yao Ming is there!

GRAMMAR TR: 69

I think Yao Ming is **the greatest** basketball player in the world.
J.K. Rowling is **the most amazing** writer I know.
In your opinion, what's **the funniest** movie of all?

4 **Read.** Complete the questions.

1. Who is ____________________ in the world? (amazing / singer)
2. In your opinion, who is ____________________? (cool / athlete)
3. What is ____________________ you watch? (interesting / TV show)
4. What is ____________________ of all? (funny / movie)

5 **What about you?** Work with a partner. Ask and answer. Complete the chart. Take turns.

Questions	Me	My partner
1. who / cool / singer		
2. what / interesting / video game		
3. who / funny / actor		
4. who / great /athlete		

6 **Listen and repeat.** Then read and match. **TR: 70**

a TV show

a hobby

a school subject

a sport

a writer

1. What's your favorite sport?
2. My parents watch a lot of boring TV shows!
3. Which country is that writer from?
4. What are your favorite hobbies?
5. What's your favorite school subject?

a. I like playing sports and going out with my friends.

b. Well, I like tennis. But I think soccer is the best.

c. I don't have one. I like all my school subjects.

d. She's from India. She's very famous.

e. My parents do, too!

7 **Work with a partner.** Stick and talk. Take turns.

I put sports first. I love soccer!

I put sports last! I don't like them.

1	2	3	4	5

GRAMMAR TR: 71

I'm **good** at music. I'm **better** than my friend at sports. And I'm **the best** in our class in English!

A cough is **bad;** a cold is **worse;** but a fever is **the worst!**

8 Complete the sentences.

I love soccer. It is ______________ free time activity of all! It's much ______________ than TV because you go out and have fun. I think TV is ______________ for your health because you don't get any exercise. And video games are ______________ because you don't learn anything!

9 **Play a game.** Cut out the cards on page 111. Play with a partner.

Cut out the cards on page 111.

What's the best sport?
I think basketball is the best.
a sport
good

10 Listen, read, and sing. TR: 72

You're the Best

I really like to play soccer.
One day I could be great!
I'll learn from my favorite athletes:
work hard, practice, and wait!

Some days I dream of fans and fame
in movies and on TV.
I study the moves of my favorite actors.
I'll be just like them, you'll see!

THE SOUNDS OF ENGLISH TR: 73

first word learn curly

11 Listen and say.

1. first thirst worst
2. word heard third
3. hurt shirt skirt
4. early curly

12 Listen and read. TR: 74

Amazing Acrobats

Most Chinese acrobats join the circus when they are six years old, but they can spend ten years practicing just one act!

a. Juggling: Acrobats use their feet to juggle things. They juggle tables, chairs, umbrellas, plates, and even people!

b. Cycling: In this act, acrobats use "monocycles" (bicycles with one wheel). The most famous act is the "bird."

c. Tight-wire: This act is about 2,000 years old. Brave acrobats walk, cycle, or jump on a wire that is high in the air.

Don't miss Chinese acrobats. They're the best!

13 Read. Label the pictures on the right *a–c*.

14 Work in a group. Compare your opinions. Write your group's decision in each box of the chart.

Acrobat Tricks			
most difficult	easiest	coolest	group favorite

I think juggling is the most difficult.
No way! Tight-wire is much more difficult.
weird but true

Some Chinese acrobats called "gastriloquists" make the sound of birds, animals, crying babies, and machines while they do their acts.

Find a role model.
Think about a person who inspires you. Why is he or she special?
NATIONAL GEOGRAPHIC
Aparajita Datta
Wildlife Biologist
Emerging Explorer
"When I was a young girl, I always wanted to be working with wildlife. But it's only because I had really great science teachers in school who gave me that interest in biology."

Bengal tiger, Bandhavgarh National Park, India

Review

1 **Listen.** How did this family live? Listen and draw lines from column A to B. TR: 75

A	B	C
We	made the fire	every day.
I	began the day at 5 a.m.	twice a day.
My dad	told funny stories	sometimes.
My grandpa	grew vegetables	on the weekend.

2 **Listen again.** How often did the family members do each activity? Draw lines from column B to C. TR: 76

3 **Write.** Prepare five questions about favorites for your classmates.

amazing	cool
popular	funny
famous	great
interesting	best / worst

actor	TV show
person	movie
hobby	vegetable
sport	athlete

4 **Work in a group.** Take turns. Ask and answer the questions you wrote. Do you share any favorite things?

What's the most amazing vegetable?
Hot peppers are the most amazing vegetables!
No way! Pumpkins are more amazing than hot peppers.

5 **Look and read.** Look at the picture below. What's wrong? Complete the sentences. Use the words in the box.

should	herself
shouldn't	himself

1. The stove is still hot. The boy ______________________ touch it.
   He can burn ______________________.
2. The knife is sharp. The girl can hurt ______________________.
3. The medicine bottle is open. Adults __________ always put away medicine.

6 **Look and read.** Read the sentences. Circle which clock each sentence is about.

a 

$14.50

b 

$19.90

c 

$40.00

d 

$45.00

1. This clock is for younger children. It's smaller than the other clock for children. **a b c d**
2. It is the most modern clock. **a b c d**
3. This one is good for children. It's more expensive than the other children's clock. **a b c d**
4. It is the most old-fashioned clock. It's the tallest, too. **a b c d**

What's wrong?

I will . . .
- ask how someone is feeling.
- describe how I feel.
- show that I care or understand.
- make a suggestion.

1 Listen and read. TR: 77

Aziz: **What's wrong?**
Sawsan: **I feel sick.**
Aziz: **Oh, no.** What's the problem?
Sawsan: I have a stomachache.
Aziz: **Why don't you** tell Mom?
Sawsan: Yeah, that's a good idea. Mom!

What's wrong?	**I feel sick.**	**Oh, no.**	**Why don't you ___?**
What's the matter?	I don't feel good. I'm not feeling well.	I'm sorry. That's too bad.	You should ___.

2 **Work with a partner.** Describe how you feel. Use the chart. Take turns.

I don't understand.

I will . . .
- politely interrupt.
- express confusion.
- check that someone understands.
- thank someone and reply.

3 Listen and read. TR: 78

Nikolai: Let's start the game.
Olga: **Hang on! I'm lost.** How do we play?
Nikolai: First, you have to spin the spinner. Then you move your counter. **Got it?**
Olga: Yeah, **I think so. Thanks.**
Nikolai: **No problem.**

Hang on! Wait. Wait a minute.	**I'm lost.** I don't understand.	**Got it?** Does that help? OK?	**I think so. Thanks.** Oh, I see! Thanks.	**No problem.** You're welcome.

4 **Listen.** You will hear two discussions. Read each question and circle the answer. TR: 79

1. Does the boy understand the instructions after the girl explains them?
   a. yes b. no
2. Which expression does the boy use?
   a. Do you see now? b. Got it? c. OK?

5 **Work in pairs.** Practice discussions. Imagine you are playing one of these games. One student doesn't understand. The other explains.

1. A card game
2. Bingo
3. A board game

Irregular Verbs

Infinitive	Simple Past	Past Participle
be	was/were	been
beat	beat	beaten
become	became	become
begin	began	begun
bend	bent	bent
bite	bit	bitten
bleed	bled	bled
blow	blew	blown
break	broke	broken
bring	brought	brought
build	built	built
buy	bought	bought
catch	caught	caught
choose	chose	chosen
come	came	come
cost	cost	cost
cut	cut	cut
dig	dug	dug
do	did	done
draw	drew	drawn
drink	drank	drunk
drive	drove	driven
eat	ate	eaten
fall	fell	fallen
feed	fed	fed
feel	felt	felt
fight	fought	fought
find	found	found
fly	flew	flown
forget	forgot	forgotten
forgive	forgave	forgiven
freeze	froze	frozen
get	got	gotten
give	gave	given
go	went	gone
grow	grew	grown
hang	hung	hung
have	had	had
hear	heard	heard
hide	hid	hidden
hit	hit	hit
hold	held	held
hurt	hurt	hurt
keep	kept	kept
know	knew	known
leave	left	left
lend	lent	lent
let	let	let
lie	lay	lain

Infinitive	Simple Past	Past Participle
light	lit	lit
lose	lost	lost
make	made	made
meet	met	met
pay	paid	paid
put	put	put
read	read	read
ride	rode	ridden
ring	rang	rung
rise	rose	risen
run	ran	run
say	said	said
see	saw	seen
sell	sold	sold
send	sent	sent
set	set	set
sew	sewed	sewn
shake	shook	shaken
shine	shone	shone
show	showed	shown
shut	shut	shut
sing	sang	sung
sink	sank	sunk
sit	sat	sat
sleep	slept	slept
slide	slid	slid
speak	spoke	spoken
spend	spent	spent
spin	spun	spun
stand	stood	stood
steal	stole	stolen
stick	stuck	stuck
sting	stung	stung
stink	stank	stunk
sweep	swept	swept
swim	swam	swum
swing	swung	swung
take	took	taken
teach	taught	taught
tear	tore	torn
tell	told	told
think	thought	thought
throw	threw	thrown
understand	understood	understood
wake up	woke up	woken up
wear	wore	worn
win	won	won
write	wrote	written

Unit 1 Let's Move TR: 7

We like to feel fit.
We like to have fun.
We like to play hard.
Let's move now, everyone!

We want to feel healthy.
We want to feel fit.
Come on, everybody.
Stand! Don't sit!

What did you do to be fit today?
What did you do to be strong?
What did you do to be fit today?
What did you do?

Did you move your legs? Yes, I did!
Did you stretch your back? I did that a lot!
Did you get enough sleep? Yes, I did!
Did you eat a healthy snack? Oops, I forgot!

Don't worry. Tomorrow is another day.
You can try again. It's OK!

We like to feel fit.
We like to have fun.
We like to play hard.
Let's jump now, everyone.

CHORUS

What did you do to be fit today?
What did you do to be strong?
What did you do to be fit today?
What did you do?

Did you stretch your muscles? Yes, I did!
Did you touch your toes? I did that a lot!
Did you bend your knees? Yes, I did!
Did you wiggle your nose? No, I forgot!

Don't worry. Tomorrow is another day.
You can try again. It's OK!

We like to feel fit.
We like to have fun.
We like to play hard.
Let's dance now, everyone.

CHORUS

Unit 2 Celebrate! TR: 16

We went to a carnival.
Everyone was there!
We dressed up, sang some songs,
and watched a parade.

But best of all,
we danced to music,
wonderful music.
We danced to music
all day long.

We danced to music,
wonderful music.
We danced to music
all day long.

Did you like the food?
Yes, I liked the food.
Did you dress up?
Yes, I went as a frog.

CHORUS

Did you like the costumes?
Yes, I liked the costumes.
Did you see any masks?
Yes, we saw some masks.

CHORUS

Unit 3 Free Time TR: 25

Free time, free time, free time is great.
There is no school, and I can sleep late.
In my free time I like to have fun.
I throw and catch. I jump and run.

What did you do on your weekend?
Did you stay at home? Did you have some fun?
What did you do on your weekend?
Did you go outside and play in the sun?

Did you go fishing?
Did you play baseball?
Did you go walking?
What did you do?

Did you go swimming?
Did you go hiking?
Did you go horseback riding?

I didn't go fishing or walking.
I didn't go swimming or hiking.
I played a game with my little brother.
I went to the movies with my mother.

CHORUS

Did you go fishing?
Did you play baseball?
Did you go walking?
What did you do?

Did you go swimming?
Did you go hiking?
Did you go horseback riding?

I stayed at home.
I played with everyone.
I lost at baseball, but it was fun.
I texted friends. I helped cook dinner.
When I help out, I feel like a winner.

CHORUS

Free time, free time, free time is great.
There is no school, and I can sleep late.
In my free time I like to have fun.
I dance and sing. I play and run.

Unit 4 We're All Different TR: 34

I'm taller than you.
He's taller than me.
We're all different.
Yes, we're different.
And I like being me!

My dad is shorter than your dad.
Your dad is younger than mine.
Our car is faster than their car.
Your car is faster than mine.
It goes fast.

CHORUS

My dog is smarter than his dog.
That dog is bigger than mine.
My dog is funnier than your dog.
It's happy all the time.

CHORUS

Unit 5 Something's Growing TR: 46

Pumpkin, lettuce, peppers, and beans.
Something's growing, and it's green.
Pumpkin, lettuce, peppers, and beans.
Something's growing, and it's green.

Working in the garden,
working in the sun,
working in the garden is a lot of fun.

I have to water the garden.
I have to weed and dig.
I look after my garden.
Those weeds grow very big!

Pumpkin, lettuce, peppers, and beans.
Something's growing, and it's green.
Pumpkin, lettuce, peppers, and beans.
Something's growing, and it's green.

We can pick cabbage in the garden.
We can pick some green beans, too.
We can plant carrots in the garden.
I like to garden, don't you?

CHORUS

Pumpkin, lettuce, peppers, and beans.
Something's growing, and it's green.
Pumpkin, lettuce, peppers, and beans.
Something's growing, and it's green.

Unit 6 Yesterday and Today TR: 54

Things were different long ago,
different in so many ways.
Things were different long ago,
different from today.

Long ago, children walked to school,
but today I ride my bike.
Long ago, we learned to sew our own clothes,
but now we buy the clothes we like.

CHORUS

We used to read by candles at night.
But now we read by electric light.
We used to talk only face-to-face.
Now we use a cell phone to call a different place.

CHORUS

People spent time with friends by the fire.
Instead, now we play video games.
But a friend is still a friend until the end.
Some things will never change!

CHORUS

Unit 7 Get Well Soon TR: 64

Take care of yourself. You know what to do.
Exercise a lot and eat the right food.
But once in a while, when you don't feel well,
here are some things that you should do.

If you have a stomachache,
you should tell your mother.
If you have a broken arm,
you should see the doctor.
If you have a toothache,
you shouldn't eat sweets.
Go to the dentist and stay away
from treats.

CHORUS

If you get a scratch from climbing a tree,
a first-aid kit will help you to take care
of your knee.
If you have a headache, you can stay in bed
or you can take some pills
to help your aching head.

Take care of yourself. You know what to do.
Exercise a lot and eat the right food.
But once in a while, when you don't feel well,
take care of yourself and get well soon!

Unit 8 You're the Best TR: 72

How do I know what I'll want one day?
How do I know what I'll be?
Who can help me to find my way
and show me how to be a better me?

I really like to play soccer.
One day I could be great!
I'll learn from my favorite athletes:
work hard, practice, and wait!

Some days I dream of fans and fame
in movies and on TV.
I study the moves of my favorite actors.
I'll be just like them, you'll see!

CHORUS

I really love the natural world:
jungles, mountains, and caves.
Like my favorite explorers,
I'll go on adventures for days and days!

I read the most talented writers,
and dream about writing a book.
I'll work very hard in school.
Becoming a writer would be so cool!

CHORUS

SUGA

take	wear	took	wore
eat	drink	ate	drank
see	sing	saw	sang
go	have	went	had

Start

after lunch	after school	tonight
on Saturday	before school	after dinner

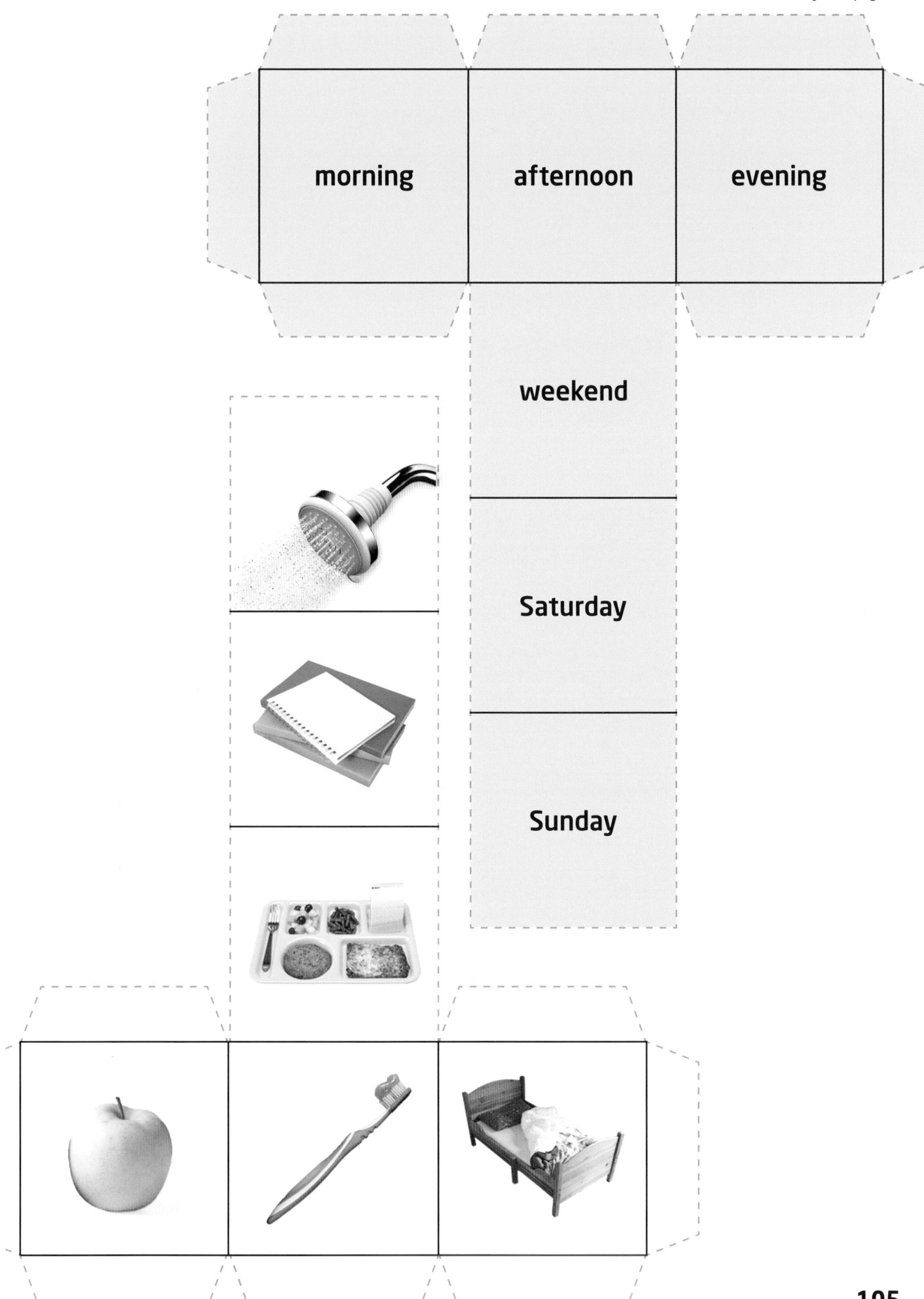
morning
afternoon
evening
weekend
Saturday
Sunday

Start

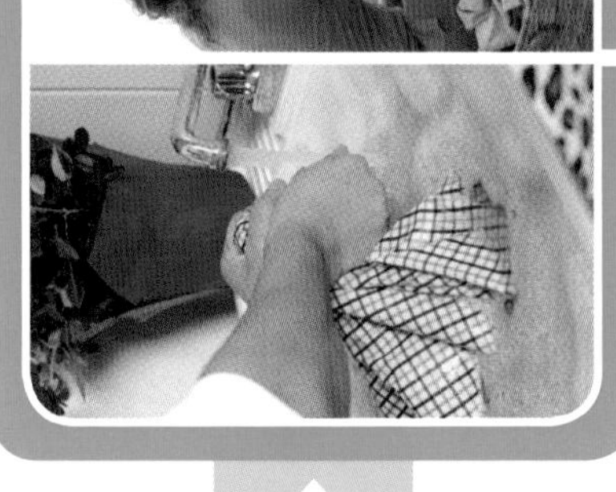

There is no electricity.
Go back two spaces.

You have to wash
clothes by hand.
Go back one space.

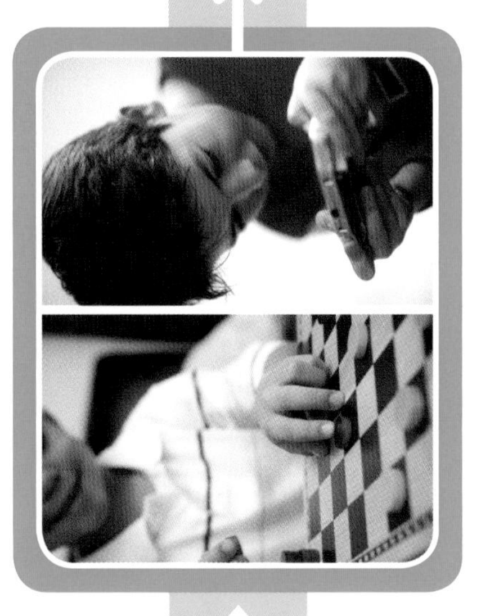

End

a famous person	food	a TV show	a school subject
a sport	a writer/book	a hobby	music/a song
interesting	cool	boring	great
good	bad	amazing	popular